CELEBRATING GOD'S CHARACTER FROM A TO Z
A CHRISTMAS DEVOTIONAL

Nickki Wiles & Rhonda Harries

outskirts
press

CELEBRATING GOD'S CHARACTER FROM A TO Z
A CHRISTMAS DEVOTIONAL
All Rights Reserved.
Copyright © 2020 Nickki Wiles & Rhonda Harries
v2.0

The opinions expressed in this manuscript are solely the opinions of the author and do not represent the opinions or thoughts of the publisher. The author has represented and warranted full ownership and/or legal right to publish all the materials in this book.

This book may not be reproduced, transmitted, or stored in whole or in part by any means, including graphic, electronic, or mechanical without the express written consent of the publisher except in the case of brief quotations embodied in critical articles and reviews.

Outskirts Press, Inc.
http://www.outskirtspress.com

ISBN: 978-1-9772-2408-8

Cover Photo © 2020 Rhonda Harries. All rights reserved - used with permission.

Outskirts Press and the "OP" logo are trademarks belonging to Outskirts Press, Inc.

PRINTED IN THE UNITED STATES OF AMERICA

"Christianity is not a doctrine to be taught, but rather a life to be lived."
Kierkegaard

Contents

How to Use This Devotional
Opening Prayer

Character Traits   Themes

Day 1	**A**lmighty	Greatest Gift	1
Day 2	**B**eckoning	Renewal	5
Day 3	**C**ompassionate	Waiting	9
Day 4	**D**eliverer	Encourage One Another	13
Day 5	**E**mpowering	Prayer	17
Day 6	**F**orgiving	Forgiveness	21
Day 7	**G**uide	Rededication	25
Day 8	**H**ealer	Restoration	29
Day 9	**I**ncredible	Witnessing	33
Day 10	**J**ehovah-Jireh	Provision	37
Day 11	**K**eeper	New Life	41
Day 12	**L**iberator	Transformation	45
Day 13	**M**erciful	Chosen	49
Day 14	**N**urturer	God's Love	53
Day 15	**O**utstanding	Self-Examination	57
Day 16	**P**rotector	Fear	61
Day 17	**Q**ualified	Humility	65
Day 18	**R**estoring	Assurance	69
Day 19	**S**acred	Promised Messiah	73
Day 20	**T**rustworthy	Remain Steadfast	77

Day 21	**U**niting	Made One in Christ	81
Day 22	**V**ictorious	Christ Centered Life	85
Day 23	**W**ise	God's Faithfulness	89
Day 24	E**X**cellent	Trust	93
Day 25	**Y**earning	Refreshment	97
Day 26	**Z**ealous	Respond to Jesus	101

For Further Study
Verses by Day

How to Use This Devotional

Our prayer is that this convenient to carry and use devotional will touch your heart in life's daily moments leading up to the celebration of Christmas. It is most challenging to keep our eyes focused on God and His character through the many distractions at this busy time of year. It's unfortunate that a season that began with God's Son as its focus has lost much of that significance. Our hope is that this devotional helps you reclaim the meaning of the gift of Christ's birth at Christmas and throughout the year. Pray for insight and direction as you read through each day. Ask God to give you a desire to make Jesus the central meaning of Christmas every year and may He help you recapture a deep all-sustaining love for your redeeming Savior.

Opening Prayer

Lord Jesus,

We ask You to come with us as we begin this journey of prayer and meditation. Open our eyes to the words You have prepared for us in Scripture. Focus our minds so we may receive Your life changing knowledge and understanding. Soften our hearts to Your presence. Help us to make room for You in this moment and throughout the weeks ahead. May our lives begin today to change for Your glory. Help us to experience the true meaning of Your saving grace and witness to those around us. Lord we give to You our mustard seed of faith, and pray You will grow the awareness, trust and love we have for You into a mighty fruitful tree. In Your glorious name we pray, Amen!

Day 1

ALMIGHTY

"God chose the lowly things of this world and the despised things, and the things that are not, to nullify the things that are, so that no one may boast before him. It is because of him that you are in Christ Jesus, who has become for us wisdom from God, that is, our righteousness, holiness and redemption. Therefore, as it is written; Let him who boasts boast in the Lord."
(1Corinthians 1: 28-31)

Almighty God gave up His greatness to take on our humanity and live our daily lives. He is no stranger to pain, sorrow and suffering. Jesus humbly came to us by way of a barn in Bethlehem. Because of Jesus, we have redemption, a clean slate and a new beginning. Do you long for a new beginning? Do you want to experience acceptance and forgiveness and leave the past behind?

Jesus wants each of us to know that forgiveness, redemption and a clean slate are available to all who come to Him. His actions prove to us that we are worthy. He demonstrated remarkable acceptance of those otherwise rejected like the Samaritan woman at the well (John 4:9). Jesus also forgave the thief on the cross and promised him eternal life (Luke 23:42-43). You may feel that you have achieved great things in your life and have earned all God has to offer, or you may find yourself feeling undeserving of His gift of love and redemption. It's not what you have done or what you haven't done. Whether you are "somebody" or feel like you are "nobody", "God demonstrates His own love for us in this: While we were still sinners, Christ died for us" (Romans 5:8). Through these example's Jesus shows us His unconditional love and acceptance. He's offering everyone who comes to Him the greatest gift of all, eternal life!

Begin this Christmas season with a fresh perspective on your relationship with Christ. Let this be a time of renewal. Praise Almighty God for all He has done for you, and all you have through Him. Open the gift of God's character from A to Z and celebrate with a grateful heart.

Dear Jesus,

We praise You **A**lmighty God. You are **A**live, and **A**ccessible to us every moment of every day. You are **A**ctive, **A**bundant and **A**ll-powerful. We can come to You with everything and **A**nything. Thank you for our sense of **A**dventure and our **A**ppetite for life. Today our hearts sing of Your **A**mazing grace. We were lost but now we're found. **A**men, **A**men!

Questions:

1. Where do you see God's "Almighty" character trait in your life?

   _____

   _____

   _____

2. Who could benefit by hearing these words of God's acceptance and love?

   _____

   _____

   _____

Reflections:

_____

_____

_____

_____

_____

_____

Day 2
BECKONING

"I know your deeds; you have a reputation of being alive but you are dead. Wake up! Strengthen what remains and is about to die, for I have not found your deeds complete in the sight of my God. Remember, therefore, what you have received and heard; obey it, and repent." (Revelation 3:1b-3)

God sent this message to the people of the church in the ancient city of Sardis. He warned them to wake up because in spite of their reputation, they were on the verge of dying. Outwardly, they appeared to be a vibrant, healthy church. But on the inside they were not. Possibly, worship had become a habit and was not heart-felt. Helping others and caring for the sick may have lost purpose and meaning. Service and tithing may have been done for recognition and not from a grateful heart. Their faith was not alive and growing.

God not only sees what we do, He knows what motivates us. He knows when our deeds are half-hearted and complacent. Like the people of Sardis, we too can experience spiritual numbness. Our participation in church can become meaningless. Bible study and prayer seems ineffective. We rely on our works instead of God's grace and become spiritually dull.

What do you do when you recognize that your spiritual life needs renewal? Put Jesus first, not just at Christmas but every day! Work to grow in your faith. Pray for a hunger for the Gospel message and read, study and meditate on it daily. Test your motives and actions to ensure your generosity and willingness to care for others flow from a heart of gratitude, not out of duty or habit. When you discover yourself falling short, repent and ask your merciful Father to breathe revival back into your dying spirit. Jesus is beckoning you to draw closer to Him. Listen intently. Wake up and be strengthened!

Lord Jesus,

You continue to **B**less us with Your presence and truth. We are thankful **B**eyond words. **B**reathe Your words of truth into our hearts and minds that we would **B**ecome alive in You. Draw us ever closer to You. In Your name we pray. Amen!

Questions:

1. What can you do to personally experience spiritual renewal?

   _____

   _____

   _____

2. Where are you challenged to serve in your church or community?

   _____

   _____

   _____

Reflections:

_____

_____

_____

_____

_____

Day 3

COMPASSIONATE

"Yet the Lord longs to be gracious to you; he rises to show you compassion. For the Lord is a God of justice. Blessed are all who wait for him!" (Isaiah 30:18)

The many demands of the Christmas season can make this time of year challenging for us. Some of us might be anticipating the joy of Christmas while others are dreading up-coming events. In any case, waiting is never easy. Isaiah tells us that we will be blessed as we wait for God and His perfect timing. The Lord desires to bless us with His grace, compassion and justice. Waiting can be part of the blessing.

Surrounded by sin and unbelief, Noah could not see God's complete plan when he was asked to build an ark (Genesis 6:14). But Noah trusted God and built the ark as the Lord instructed him. Noah, his family, and the animals, lived on the cramped, uncomfortable ark for over 150 days as the rain fell. Surely they prayed daily for the Lord to save them but God's answer was the same for Noah and his family as it sometimes is for us…wait!

Possibly, you find yourself in an uncomfortable period of waiting for test results, a long desired pregnancy, a new job or a lasting relationship. It's easy to overlook the Lord drawing you closer to Him in the anxiety of waiting. If you are not open to His plan of waiting, it's impossible to experience the fullest measure of His compassion and grace.

What are we to do as we wait on the Lord? Be strong and let your heart take courage (Psalm 27:14). Draw strength from others who have experienced a similar situation of waiting. Focus on God's love instead of your desired answer to prayer. An unexpected note or gift from someone or even a sweet smile or glance can remind you of God's love as you wait patiently. We are waiting but God is working! Take time to pause and meet Jesus daily and often. Love and care for those the Lord puts in your path and enjoy each moment given to you. Be uplifted, encouraged and reach out to others. Savor joyous times and experience God's grace, comfort and strength through every challenge. Watch expectantly for the Lord your God throughout this season of waiting. You will receive the blessing He promises as you wait for Him.

Christ Jesus,

You are Compassionate, Comforting and full of grace. It is Crucial that we slow down so You can Care for us. Create in us the desire to wait expectantly this Christmas season and throughout the coming year. In good times and bad, You are our Companion. We pray to be Consumed by Your love as we wait Your perfect timing. Come Lord Jesus, Come. Amen!

Questions:

1. What are you longing for God to do in your life?

_____

_____

_____

2. How can you draw closer to God at this time and trust His perfect timing for the answers you desire?

_____

_____

_____

Reflections:

_____

_____

_____

_____

_____

_____

Day 4

*D*ELIVERER

"For the Lord himself will come down from heaven, with a loud command, with the voice of the archangel and with the trumpet call of God, and the dead in Christ will rise first. After that, we who are still alive and are left will be caught up together with them in the clouds to meet the Lord in the air. And so we will be with the Lord forever. Therefore, encourage each other with these words." (1Thessalonians 4:16-18)

Paul writes these words in his letter to the church at Thessalonica. These words are encouraging for us as well. They reveal how Jesus will draw us to Himself in the end times. Picture this scene; a commanding trumpet call, the dead rising up, the Lord appearing in the sky and people caught up together to meet Him in the air. Sounds like a Spielberg masterpiece, a movie or someone's imagination come to life on the screen. It is a masterpiece, God's masterpiece! The deliverance described here gives us great hope for living each day. The promise of seeing someone you have loved and lost can comfort an otherwise troubled heart.

    Christmas can be a joyful time of year for many but some silently suffer through the season. Has this been a tough year for you? Are you mourning the loss of someone close? Be encouraged! You will see them again. If you've not lost a loved one, who do you know that could benefit from the truth of these verses? The Lord did not intend for us to walk through tough times alone. "He comes alongside us when we go through hard times, and before you know it, He brings us alongside someone else who is going through hard times so that we can be there for that person just as God was there for us" (2 Corinthians 1:3-5 MSG). At Christmas, we celebrate Jesus coming as our Savior and one day soon, He will return as our divine Deliverer. In the meantime, we are to encourage one another with the comfort that only God's truth can give.

Dearest Lord Jesus,

You offer us **D**eliverance from the **D**epth of our **D**espair, and we can **D**ance in the knowledge that You are in control. As light **D**estroys **D**arkness, sin and **D**eath are being **D**estroyed in Your **D**ivine presence. Our hope is in You, Jesus. You are our **D**ependable **D**eliverer. As our **D**evotion to You grows, show us how to encourage others with these **D**efining truths: You are the light of the world. You have come to save us all. Praise be to God; Father, Son and Holy Spirit. Amen!

Questions:

1. How do these verses about Christ's return influence the way you live?

   _____

   _____

   _____

2. How are you comforted by these verses?

   _____

   _____

   _____

Reflections:

_____

_____

_____

_____

_____

Day 5

*E*MPOWERING

"With this in mind, we constantly pray for you, that our God may count you worthy of his calling, and that by his power he may fulfill every good purpose of yours and every act prompted by your faith. We pray this so that the name of our Lord Jesus may be glorified in you, and you in him, according to the grace of our God and the Lord Jesus Christ." (2 Thessalonians 1:11-12)

Throughout the New Testament, Jesus shows us the importance of having an open conversation with His Heavenly Father (Mark 11:25; Luke 6:12, and 11:1-13). When we spend time in converstion with God, we become acutely aware of His presence. We grow closer to God and begin to hear Him speak to our hearts. By His teaching, directing and comforting, we become empowered to continually seek Him through prayer. This connects our relationship with Him in a deep and personal way.

When we ask God to help those we know and care about, we will be privileged to witness the Lord work in their lives. This grows our trust for Jesus into a deeper level of intimacy. The Holy Spirit knows what each of us needs and He helps us as we pray. Our desire to talk to the Lord will increase as our prayer life grows.

If someone comes to mind, take a minute and pray for them and continue as long as they remain on your heart. Send a note of encouragement to remind them you care and are thinking about them. Jesus spoke to your heart, you prayed and someone was blessed. Out of your gratitude, praise Him!

This Christmas and beyond, devote yourself to prayer as He prompts you. Pray to the Lord for your personal needs and the needs of those you love. Remember those you know and those you don't know in prayer. Continue this habit into the new year. Be empowered to live a life of prayer!

Most Excellent Lord Jesus,

You Empower us through Your Spirit to pray. Grow our understanding that our prayer can be Effective. Continue to teach us to pray Earnestly for others. We praise You and Eagerly wait for Your continued guidance and prompting to pray Each and Every day. To You be the glory. Amen!

Questions:

1. Do you believe prayer is powerful? Why or why not?

   _____

   _____

   _____

2. How can you pray more effectively?

   _____

   _____

   _____

Reflections:

_____

_____

_____

_____

_____

_____

Day 6

*F*ORGIVING

"Jesus said, 'Father, forgive them, for they do not know what they are doing.'" (Luke 23:34)

Jesus forgave His captors while they were still actively abusing Him. They betrayed, beat, mocked and taunted Him repeatedly. Those closest to Him were no exception. Peter denied knowing Him (Luke 22:54-62), Thomas doubted His resurrection (John 20:24-28), and Judas betrayed Him (Matthew 26:47-59). Jesus illustrates clearly our Lord's profound ability to forgive in the most extreme circumstances. He recognized the freedom that comes through forgiveness.

How long do you hold onto your hurt and anger? When someone intentionally or unintentionally causes you harm, are you quick to forgive or do you hold a grudge waiting for an apology. Our unwillingness to extend forgiveness or apologize causes the pain inside to consume us. True unconditional forgiveness and genuine apologies will transform your life as you learn to follow Jesus.

You may feel the offense against you is impossible to forgive. Jesus understands. He suffered death and the grave because of the heartless acts of others. He forgave them and He forgives us the same way. Pray for a heart that's quick to forgive and eyes that recognize the hurt you've caused others. Extend forgiveness in even the most difficult circumstances and receive the peace that surpasses all understanding. This peace is the greatest gift of all.

Dear Lord,

You are our Forgiving Father. You are Faithful to Fulfill Your promises and You Fiercely love Your children. You are more than our Friend. You are our Savior, our Comforter, our Confidant and we are Forever grateful. Fill us with Your grace. In Your name Jesus we pray. Amen!

Questions:

1. Who has hurt you deeply and needs your unconditional forgiveness?

_____

_____

2. Why should you be quick to forgive like Jesus?

_____

_____

Reflections:

_____

_____

_____

_____

_____

Day 7

*G*UIDE

"Now I, King Artaxerxes, order all the treasures of Trans-Euphrates to provide with diligence whatever Ezra the priest, a teacher of the Law of the God of heaven, may ask of you, up to a hundred talents of silver, a hundred cors of wheat, a hundred baths of wine, a hundred baths of olive oil, and salt without limit. Whatever the God of heaven has prescribed, let it be done with diligence for the temple of the God of heaven." (Ezra 7:21-23)

God told the Israelites exactly what to do and how to do it. He tells us in these verses that whatever He asks of us, we are to do with diligence. We are called to tirelessly follow the Lord, with close attention and perseverance. Ancient architecture reminds us that years ago people took great pride in what they built. They would carve intricate designs into places that might not be noticed. Today this level of attention and detail can often be over looked.

This can be witnessed in all walks of life. Some remain dedicated to their calling and continue their work to the end. They get little or no recognition and yet they continually and meticulously give their time and talents, blessing many around them. They are true witnesses of a faithful servant of God. Getting paid and recognized by others for what we are doing can be satisfying, but the recognition we receive from Jesus is more rewarding. We can learn from these faithful servants that whatever we do, do it to the glory of God (1 Corinthians 10:31).

We are witnessing to future generations by our determination and dedication. Doing whatever we do with diligence, even if no one is watching, brings glory to God. Jesus sees all, and one day we will hear him say; "Well done good and faithful servant" (Matthew 25:23). This Christmas season, rededicate yourself to a chosen task using God alone as your guide to completion. Faithfully follow God's calling, pray consistently, and pay careful attention to all that you do as you seek His guidance.

Father **G**od,

You have been **G**racious with us, and You call us to be **G**enerous with our time and the **G**ifts You have given us. Out of **G**ratitude, we will do our best to be diligent in everything we do. **G**uide us with Your Spirit of **G**race, to persevere for Your **G**lory. In Jesus name we pray. Amen!

Questions:

1. What unfinished task are you challenged to complete with excellence?

   _____

   _____

   _____

2. How can you specifically pray for God's guidance?

   _____

   _____

   _____

Reflections:

_____

_____

_____

_____

_____

Day 8
*H*EALER

"Blessed are those whose strength is in you, who have set their hearts on pilgrimage. As they pass through the Valley of Baca, they make it a place of springs; the autumn rains also cover it with pools. They go from strength to strength, till each appears before God in Zion." (Psalm 84:5-7)

    As the Israelites traveled on their pilgrimage to worship in Jerusalem, they passed through an area known as the Valley of Baca. The King James Version calls this area the "Valley of Weeping". The discomfort the travelers endured in this dry, sterile, waterless land would diminish as they experienced joy in worship and fellowship with other believers at their destination. The dry valley of hardship and suffering was transformed into a place of soul refreshment and healing as they trusted God's strength to complete their journey.

    Many of us are traveling through our own personal Valley of Baca. Hurt or betrayal can instantly place us in a dry and lonely valley. A rebellious child, rejection by a friend or a spouse, a sudden loss or tragedy can drain us of all joy and strength. When life's problems descend, where do you turn? Do you rely on your knowledge, finances or profession to be your source of strength and hope? Or do you choose to put your trust in God alone?

Make a decision today to move through life's challenges with your strength in the Lord, our healer. He can transform sorrow and the most painful losses into blessings. The prophet Zechariah reminds us, "Return to your fortress O prisoners of hope; even now I announce that I will restore twice as much to you" (Zechariah 9:12). Our healing God is able to return double our loss and bring lasting joy to our broken hearts. Open yourself to the restoration Jesus gives and look up with anticipation to the star over Bethlehem as you continue to move forward in faith.

Holy Lord,

You are our **H**elp when we are weak. You bring **H**ealing to our **H**eavy **H**earts. As we journey through this life toward **H**eaven You Lord, give us the strength we long for. We are **H**umbled and grateful for all the ways You love us. **H**allowed be Your **H**oly name. Amen, Come Lord Jesus. Amen!

Questions:

1. Where are you feeling pain or betrayal leaving you in your own personal Valley of Baca?

   _____

   _____

   _____

2. How have you found God's comfort?

   _____

   _____

   _____

Reflections:

_____
_____
_____
_____
_____

Day 9

*I*NCREDIBLE

"At this they wept again. Then Orpah kissed her mother-in-law good-by, but Ruth clung to her. 'Look,' said Naomi, 'your sister-in-law is going back to her people and her gods. Go back with her.' But Ruth replied, 'Don't urge me to leave you or to turn back from you. Where you go I will go, and where you stay I will stay. Your people will be my people and your God my God.' " (Ruth 1:14-16)

Naomi suffered the loss of her husband. Her daughters-in-law watched how she lived. They saw something in Naomi they didn't see in their own people. She kept it together when her sons died, even though she was in severe anguish and pain. There was something in Naomi that Ruth wasn't willing to walk away from. That something was her God. Naomi was hurt and feeling abandoned but she never stopped believing in the one true God. Ruth did not want to return to the empty way of life she had before she knew Yahweh.

In our struggles and loss, we too have experienced Yahweh...God with us. God provides for us, comforts us and guides us. Like Naomi, it's okay to be angry, hurt, frustrated and disappointed but when you know Jesus, you are never alone or without hope. Those we know and meet will want to go where we go, and stay where we stay because of our witness. Through the light of Jesus in us, they see Christ. Pray that in every circumstance, God's great love would be revealed in your example. And those we love, along with others who haven't yet experienced the Lord's love, would one day say, "Your people will be my people and your God my God." Our God is so incredible; He is in the business of miracles. May the coming Christ reveal Himself to others through each one of us.

Jesus,

You are Incredible. We have joy Inside us because You reside in our hearts. Impress Your love upon us in such a way that we would Influence others by our witness. We pray that they would be Inspired to go where You go and stay where You stay. Ignite in us Your Spirit's flame so we would be a beacon of love for Christ's glory. In Jesus name we pray. Amen!

Questions:

1. Who do you look to for strength when you are suffering?

   _____

   _____

   _____

2. How does Naomi's example challenge or encourage you?

   _____

   _____

   _____

Reflections:

_____
_____
_____
_____
_____

Day 10

JEHOVAH-JIREH

Jesus said, "Come to me all you who are weary and burdened, and I will give you rest. Take my yoke upon you and learn from me, for I am gentle and humble in heart, and you will find rest for your souls. For my yoke is easy and my burden is light." (Matthew 11:28-30)

God's provision for His people is evident throughout Scripture. He supplied a ram for Abraham as he was about to sacrifice his son, Isaac. Abraham called the name of the place of sacrifice Jehovah-Jireh, which means the Lord will provide (Genesis 22:13-14 KJV). God protected Joseph multiple times as he was sold into slavery, brought into Egypt, and thrown into prison (Genesis 37:28-39:20). In spite of many challenges, He was delivered from his trials, forgave his brothers and cared for many. Regardless of opposition, Joseph boldly praised God for providing all he needed (Genesis 50:20-21). Even the starving Israelites were fed manna daily as they wandered through the desert (Exodus 16:15).

Jesus too experienced His Father's rich provision. Ministering angels were sent to Him after He was tempted by the devil (Matthew 4:11). As Jesus sweat drops of blood in Gethsemane an angel appeared and strengthened Him in His agony (Luke 22:43-44). Jesus prayed even more earnestly and was provided the strength He needed to carry our sins to the cross.

We also can experience God's generous supply for our weary souls. God will provide for all our needs as He becomes our Jehovah-jireh. He gives us Jesus, the Bread of Life, to sustain us. He comforts us with His chosen family and friends. Jehovah-jireh fills our cup to overflowing as we embrace Him. Lean in close to the manger and receive His abundant provision for your weary soul today and every day.

Lord Jesus,

You are Just what we need in every situation. Though our lives are stressed and Jam packed You provide for us and we find rest in You alone. You desire to bring us Joy. Help us to Jump at the chance to come when You call. We place ourselves and those we love in Your humble yet mighty hands. In Your name Jesus we pray. Amen!

Questions:

1. Where in your life have you experienced God's generous blessings?

   _____

   _____

   _____

2. What specific challenge do you need to give to God?

   _____

   _____

   _____

Reflections:

_____

_____

_____

_____

_____

_____

Day 11
*K*EEPER

"The word of the Lord came to me: 'Go and proclaim in the hearing of Jerusalem; I remember the devotion of your youth, how as a bride you loved me and followed me through the desert, through a land not sown.'" (Jeremiah 2:1-2)

The Lord remembers with fondness how we loved him when we first came to know him. We were completely devoted to Him, eager to study the Bible, go to church and share our new-found faith with others. Out of that same love, the Israelites left what was familiar and followed the Lord through the desert, a land unknown. By day God guided them in a pillar of cloud and at night in a pillar of fire (Exodus 13:21-22).

With Jesus as our Shepherd, we too can travel new territory together. We can follow Him away from the former life we were living, into a life of forgiveness and grace. Moving forward won't always be easy. New patterns, habits and friendships will develop. The one constant will be Jesus, our Keeper. Remain devoted to Him and He will give you strength (Philippians 4:13). He is our trustworthy companion, walking before us. He is beside us holding us up and carrying us when necessary.

It's tempting to look back with longing to our old life. It can even be immobilizing. Pray for courage to let it go! Put on your new self, created in the likeness of God (Ephesians 4:22-24). Remain steady and move forward with Jesus. As you head into the new year, take His hand and go where He leads you. It will be hard at times but with determination and trust, God will surprise you with a deep rewarding relationship with Him.

Jesus,

You are our **K**eeper, our constant companion. You **K**now what we need and You provide us with Your loving care. You Jesus are the **K**ey to what our longing heart's desire. Shine Your light into our lives today. We pray for all those who find this time of year challenging and ask You to **K**indly reveal Your love to them. In Your name Jesus, our **K**ing of **K**ings we pray. Amen!

Questions:

1. How have you changed recently in your devotional habits?

   _____

   _____

   _____

2. What can you leave behind to grow closer to God?

   _____

   _____

   _____

Reflections:
_____
_____
_____
_____
_____
_____

Day 12

ℒ*IBERATOR*

"'Even now,' declares the Lord, 'return to me with all your heart, with fasting and weeping and mourning.' Rend your heart and not your garments. Return to the Lord your God, for he is gracious and compassionate, slow to anger and abounding in love, and he relents from sending calamity." (Joel 2:12-13)

Has your relationship with God been a significant part of your life this past year? Or, is He only important to you at Christmas, Easter or when you are in need? What keeps you from moving closer to the Lord in your daily life? The list of excuses is endless: priorities, schedules, personal choices and interruptions to name a few. Are you okay with that?

Whether you've been walking with Him faithfully for years or had a relationship full of stumbles along the way, in this verse, Jesus is calling you to return to Him. He declares, "Return to me with all your heart." It's never too late to change your life! He alone can liberate you from your sin and help you make a fresh start.

Where do we begin? Ask forgiveness and make a conscious effort to move closer to Him. Physically get out your Bible, open it and pray for guidance. Consider Paul who called himself, "Public Sinner Number One" (1 Timothy 1:15-16 MSG). He experienced regret for his past. Read how the Lord's generous mercy liberated him. Use Paul's example for a radical change and make a personal plan to move forward. Write down your steps to change and put them into action. Thank God for His compassion and grace to cleanse you as you turn to Him with all your heart. Then confidently move forward to make these daily changes that will liberate you from your past. There is no better time for transformation than now.

Lord Jesus,

    We look forward to the day You return with both trepidation and Longing. Give us all the strength we need to cling fast to You until that day. Your patience with us is Long Lasting. For You Lord, Live to Lavish Your Love upon us. Hallelujah, Come Lord Jesus, Amen!

Questions:

1. What challenges you most about this day's reading?

_____

_____

_____

2. What impact has this devotional had on your life?

_____

_____

_____

Reflections:

_____

_____

_____

_____

_____

_____

Day 13

ℳERCIFUL

"For the Lord your God is a merciful God, he will not abandon or destroy you or forget the covenant with your forefathers, which He confirmed to them by oath." (Deuteronomy 4:31)

Do you sometimes feel abandoned and forgotten? You are not alone. There are countless examples in the Bible of God's people feeling hopeless and deserted. At age 75, childless Abraham was told by God He would become a great nation. Many years later, at the age of 100, God's promise was finally fulfilled through Isaac (Genesis 21:1-5). David was guilty of both adultery and murder (2 Samuel 11:1-17) yet was forever recorded in Scripture as the man after God's own heart (Acts 13:22). Widowed Ruth left home and family to seek Naomi's God (Ruth 1:16). She not only became David's great grand-mother; she's listed in the lineage of Jesus (Matthew 1:5). In these instances, and others recorded in Scripture, God showed His abundant mercy to people just like you and me.

Perhaps you are struggling with sin like David. You know you are forgiven but persistent thoughts and desires have a hold on you. You feel like you are never good enough. Years were passing Abraham by with still no promised heir. Pressured by Sara, he took the situation in his own hands instead of waiting for God's timing. We can find ourselves doing the same thing. Ruth was a widow with no hope of a family of her own. Clinging to God as her Father her family grew to include not only King David but our Savior.

If you have been waiting for an answer to the same prayer request for years or feel guilty of unforgivable sin, these Bible verses are for you. Examine each one of them and be encouraged. Our God has a history of keeping His promises, doing the impossible and providing abundant mercy to the undeserving. Cry out to the Lord.

He has not abandoned or forgotten you (Psalm 116:1). He has chosen you as His own. God, in His abundant mercy provided His long-awaited Son to cleanse us from our sins. God's provision of mercy, forgiveness and belonging has come to us through His Son, our Savior Jesus Christ.

Lord Jesus,

You are **M**ighty and **M**erciful. You give us strength for today and hope for tomorrow. We can work to **M**anipulate and **M**anufacture things to go as we want them, but You are not **M**isled by our **M**aneuvers. We are not the **M**asters of our universe. **M**ercifully, You forgive us all our sins. You love us without **M**easure, like a **M**other loves her child. We are grateful for Your constant presence in our lives. Amen!

Questions:

1. Where have you seen God's mercy in your life?

   _____

   _____

   _____

2. Which biblical hero are you challenged to study further?

   _____

   _____

   _____

Reflections:

_____
_____
_____
_____
_____
_____

Day 14

Nurturer

"The Lord appeared to us in the past, saying: 'I have loved you with an everlasting love; I have drawn you with loving-kindness.'" (Jeremiah 31:3)

    This promise of everlasting love in Jeremiah was made to all Israel as God's chosen people. The same promise of God's loyal covenant love is ours today and throughout eternity. The theme of God's love encompasses the Bible from beginning to end. From the fall of man in Genesis to complete restoration in Revelation, God repeatedly shows man His unconditional, nurturing love. God's love is the only love that is complete and perfect, delivered with a guarantee and sealed in the blood of Christ. His love leads us, feeds us, protects us and will never fail (Psalm 136). "This is the kind of love we are talking about, not that we once upon a time loved God but that He loved us and sent His Son as a sacrifice to clear away our sins and the damage they have done to our relationship with God" (1John 4:10 MSG).

God's extravagant love is meant to be shared and we are called to demonstrate that same love (John 13:34-35). If you are thinking, "I could never love like Jesus loves," you are right. But, if you personally know the love of God through a relationship with Him, you can generously share that gift with others, especially at Christmas.

Do you believe you are personally loved and chosen by Christ? If the answer is "no", you can discover through the pages of Scripture that His love is like no other love you have ever experienced. In time, you will grow to know the deep satisfaction that only the love of God can give. If your response is "yes", then help others to truly understand God's love through an abundance of acceptance, forgiveness and generosity. Nurture others as you have been nurtured by God. Seek to repair relationships and find opportunities to demonstrate unity and unconditional love. Show others the Lord's love and when someone asks them, "How do you know God loves you personally?", they will say, "I experienced the love of God by the generous ways His disciples have loved me."

Loving God,

You are always **N**ear to us even when we are far from You. You **N**urture us and Your love endures forever. **N**ight and day You are drawing us ever closer to You. We are in **N**eed of Your saving grace. Make us **N**ew in You. In Jesus **N**ame we pray. Amen!

Questions:

1. What eternal significance does Jeremiah 31:3 have on you?

   _____

   _____

   _____

2. Who in your life needs your acceptance and generosity?

   _____

   _____

   _____

Reflections:

Day 15

*O*UTSTANDING

"Is not my house right with God? Has he not made with me an everlasting covenant, arranged and secured in every part? Will he not bring to fruition my salvation and grant me my every desire?" (2 Samuel 23:5)

King David's final words clearly reveal his struggle to live a righteous life. Adultery with Bathsheba, murder and cover-up of her husband Uriah's death, and a household full of conflict were part of David's past. His struggles, sorrows, and sins were many and his kingdom was full of opposition. Our lives can also reveal a past full of difficulty, but like David we have a choice of where to place our focus. He chose to focus on God's everlasting covenant and future salvation yet to come. Advent is the perfect opportunity to examine our hearts and refocus our attitude on our future in Christ's kingdom.

Is your heart right with God? Do others know Jesus is the center of your life? Do your actions and words reflect your love of Christ? At Christmas time the answer to many of these questions is most likely "yes". What about the other seasons of the year? People should always see and experience a difference in us. In spite of opposition, discouragement and disappointment, we are able to persevere because of our eternal perspective. The way we live and love plants seeds of faith in other's hearts. In God's perfect timing, He can and will fertilize and grow their faith.

Give your heart to Him and focus on a future with Him, instead of earthly things. Make spending time in prayer and thanksgiving a priority in your life. Pray and witness both silently and openly. Trust the Lord will bring to fruition your salvation and the salvation of those you pray for. And when you ask yourself, "Is my heart, my home, and my house right with God?", the answer will be "yes", because our outstanding Lord has made an everlasting covenant arranged and secured in every part, through Jesus Christ our Lord and Savior.

Outstanding Father,

You are **O**mniscient, knowing everything. You are **O**mnipotent; all powerful. You love us completely and we are **O**vercome with gratitude. Teach us to stand **O**ut for You. Make **O**ur hearts **O**pen and right with You. In Jesus' name we pray. Amen!

Questions:

1. What action plan can you put into place that will make a significant difference in your personal life?

   _____

   _____

   _____

2. What obstacles will you face as you follow this plan?

   _____

   _____

   _____

Reflections:

_____

_____

_____

_____

_____

Day 16

Protector

"I took you from the ends of the earth, from its farthest corners I called you. I said, 'You are my servant; I have chosen you and have not rejected you. So do not fear, for I am with you; do not be dismayed, for I am your God. I will strengthen you and help you; I will uphold you with my righteous right hand.'" (Isaiah 41:9-10)

The first recorded example of fear in the Bible is when Adam and Eve hid from God in the garden because they were afraid (Genesis 3:10). Fear and anxiety have been part of our world from the beginning. There are many examples throughout Scripture of people who were fearful. When the Israelites finally arrived at the promised land, they sent out men to explore this new territory. The explorers returned with proof of abundant fruit but also a report of powerful people and fortified cities (Numbers 13). This news spread among the Israelites causing panic. Consequently, not one of the Israelites over twenty years old entered the promised land except

Caleb and Joshua. Fear had caused the people to doubt God's promise in spite of His miraculous provisions for them. He had fed them and protected them throughout their travels yet they failed to believe His promise that they would live and prosper in this new land.

We all experience anxiety and fear, which can take over our thoughts and appear impossible to overcome. Job related problems, family issues, a sudden illness, moving or retirement can cause distress and concern. Fear can stop us in our tracks and paralyze us. How can we overcome fear and place our trust in God when we face challenging situations?

Fix our eyes on Him as we step out in faith. God's words of assurance can be our constant hope in our moments of uncertainty. He wants us to know that He will strengthen us and help us in these situations. Fear is natural to us but His perfect love drives out fear (1John 4:18). God has chosen us, He will strengthen and protect us and hold us upright with His right hand. We have His constant support. He will not reject us. The next time you are unsettled and feel anxious, trust this powerful verse and God's everlasting promise of protection for you.

Lord Jesus,

You are our **P**rince of **P**eace. You have **P**ersonally **P**icked each of us and given us the **P**rivilege to **P**roclaim You to those around us. **P**lease, **P**rovide us with **P**erfect opportunities to share Your **P**owerful word to others. Give us Your **P**assion and **P**erception as to when and where to **P**resent the truth of Your **P**resence in our lives. Grant us continued **P**rotection, as we **P**atiently trust and wait for Your **P**romised return. We **P**raise You and **P**ray in Your most **P**recious name. Amen!

Questions:

1. What specific fear can God help you let go of today?

_____

_____

_____

2. Where do you need God's protection during this Christmas season?

_____

_____

_____

Reflections:

_____

_____

_____

_____

_____

_____

Day 17
QUALIFIED

"Your attitude should be the same as that of Christ Jesus: Who being in very nature God, did not consider equality with God something to be grasped, but made himself nothing, taking the very nature of a servant, being made in human likeness. And being found in appearance as a man, he humbled himself and became obedient to death, even death on a cross!" (Philippians 2:5-8)

When we look to Jesus, we see an example of unsurpassed humility. He voluntarily chose homelessness and associated with the common people that those in authority disregarded. He remained silent in the face of His accusers, Pilate and Herod (Matthew 27:12-14; Luke 23:9). Jesus took the role of a servant and washed His disciples' feet (John 13:4-17). He demonstrated that humility is not a sign of weakness but strength. Jesus challenges us to do as He does promising we will be blessed through our actions.

Humility does not come naturally to us. It's more natural to point out others faults and failures drawing attention away from our own shortcomings. We justify our actions rather than remain silent and desire to associate with influential people. The choice of humility is not only unnatural for us, it's costly. Our position, respect and prestige matter to us.

When we choose to exalt ourselves, we fail to recognize our need for a Savior. Jesus alone is qualified like no other. He extends His forgiveness and grace to each of us. Pray we find it within ourselves to extend His grace to others. Christmas is the perfect time to humble yourself and give unpredictably. Look for people you can bless anonymously with generosity. Your list can include your postman, grocery cashier, local homeless shelter and elderly neighbor. Who can you unexpectedly give to in an act of kindness or service this season and throughout the new year?

Dear Lord,

You are **Q**uick to forgive. Sadly, we are slow. We can be loud and judgmental of others and You are **Q**uiet and compassionate. We **Q**uestion people's motives becoming **Q**uarrelsome over the smallest things. Not holding our sins against us, You **Q**uench our thirst with Your living water. Wash us of our sins and **Q**uicken in us Your Spirit, giving us the desire to be accepting of others as You are with us. Come **Q**uickly Lord Jesus. Amen!

Questions:

1. How does Jesus' example of humility challenge you?

   _____
   _____
   _____

2. Which other character trait of Jesus can you show by example to others?

   _____
   _____
   _____

Reflections:

Day 18
ℛESTORING

*"The Lord is my shepherd, I shall not be in want. He makes me lie down in green pastures, he leads me beside quiet waters, he restores my soul. He guides me in the paths of righteousness for his name's sake. Even though I walk through the valley of the shadow of death, I will fear no evil, for you are with me; your rod and your staff, they comfort me." (*Psalm 23:1-4*)*

The Bible gives many examples of God's restorative nature. All of Psalm 23 illustrates His power to lead, refresh, guide and comfort His people. Jesus comforted the sorrowful, healed the broken and befriended the rejected. One of the most powerful examples is the woman caught in adultery yet forgiven by Jesus. The Pharisees were ready to condemn her and have her stoned but Jesus lovingly forgave her and asked her to leave her life of sin (John 8: 3-11). Instantly, she had new life.

The woman Jesus saved gained everything through her encounter with Him. We can too! Are you feeling rejected and undeserving? Today is the perfect time to ponder God's gift to you, His Son. Devote a few moments to your own personal mini-retreat with God. Have an extended quiet time, several minutes of additional prayer or choose a hymn to sing that opens your heart to the opportunity of the Lord's healing power. Journal this time with God and refer to it when you feel a sense of loss and sorrow replacing the joy of Christ's birth. Jesus' restorative power will change and heal you as you experience God's love in a new and fresh way.

What you think is lost can be restored through God's healing. We cannot comprehend what God has in store for us. He is able to do immeasurably more than all we ask or imagine, according to his power that is at work within us (Ephesians 3:20). Discover the new life Jesus has for you today.

Radiant Lord,

You are **R**emarkable. You have **R**econciled us through Your loving sacrifice. Your love **R**ichly **R**ains down on us every day. **R**eleasing us from the **R**estraints of our sin. **R**estore our **R**elationship with You through Your grace in Jesus Christ, our **R**edeemer. May we **R**ecognize Your deep **R**eassuring love for us and **R**emain **R**ooted in Your peace and comfort. In Your **R**ighteous name Jesus, we pray. Amen!

Questions:

1. How is God restoring our world today?

   _____

   _____

   _____

2. Where have you experienced God's restorative power in your life?

   _____

   _____

   _____

Reflections:

_____

_____

_____

_____

_____

_____

Day 19

*S*ACRED

"Therefore, the Lord himself will give you a sign: The virgin will be with child and will give birth to a son, and will call him Immanuel." (Isaiah 7:14)

The Lord gave us a sign through Isaiah that a son would be born to a virgin and His name would be Immanuel, God with us. 700 years later God's promise came to fruition in the birth of Jesus Christ. But many did not make the connection to the promised Messiah, even though the signs were evident. They heard the prophecies and saw Jesus but chose not to believe. Like those before us, we too can ignore obvious proof and miss the opportunity to recognize Jesus and see the truth.

Birds flying south is evidence that winter is coming. Dark heavy clouds indicate rain is inevitable. And contractions confirm the baby is soon to come. We've been reading and interpreting signs for years. But do we recognize the biblical prophecy that God gives us pointing to the truth of His Son, our Savior? His lineage was foretold beginning with Abraham through King David and recorded in His genealogy in Matthew 1. The birthplace of Bethlehem was prophesied by the prophet Micah (Micah 5:2). The wise men followed the star in the East in search of the newborn King because they knew the Old Testament prophecies and recognized the signs (Matthew 2:1-2). There was ample confirmation that Jesus was the Son of God, the promised Savior.

God has given the whole world evidence. Old Testament prophecy was perfectly fulfilled in the recorded life of Jesus Christ. The virgin gives birth to a son, Jesus lives a holy sacred life (Hebrews 4:15), heals the sick (Luke 7:22), feeds the hungry and dies on a cross for our sins. Throughout Scripture, we learn that Jesus is the promised Savior. Pray for eyes to see, ears to hear and a heart that understands. He's not taking a long time coming. Jesus is patiently waiting for us to see the ever-present signs, to understand them, and believe. This Christmas, boldly share the message prophesied long ago with others.

Holy, Sacred Savior,

You have come to Shine Your light Straight into our hearts. You Lord, are our Shepherd. We are Safe in Your arms. We have been made Spotless through Your Sacrifice. Sin no longer has power over our lives. We are Stamped with Your Holy Spirit. Satan may Seek to Shake us but with You as our Strong, Solid foundation, nothing or no one can Separate us from Your Sheltering love. Give us eyes to See the Signs, ears to hear and a voice to Sing praises to You. Amen!

Questions:

1. Which biblical prophecies challenge you the most?

　
　
　

2. Who in your life needs to hear these truths?

Reflections:

_____

_____

_____

_____

_____

_____

Day 20

TRUSTWORTHY

"Do you not know? Have you not heard? The Lord is the everlasting God, the Creator of the ends of the earth. He will not grow tired or weary, and his understanding no one can fathom. He gives strength to the weary and increases the power of the weak. Even youths grow tired and weary, and young men stumble and fall; but those who hope in the Lord will renew their strength. They will soar on wings like eagles; they will run and not grow weary, they will walk and not be faint." (Isaiah 40:28-31)

In these verses, Isaiah is responding to the Israelites complaints that God doesn't care about them. They see surrounding nations who have more resources and they are convinced that God has abandoned their needs. Despite the miracles of water from a rock, daily manna, and lasting provisions for generations before them, their faith had weakened to the point of not trusting His promises. Like the Israelites, we too have doubts and question God.

How do we keep steadfast when our heart's desires remain unfulfilled? We long for a steady income, protected health, home and family, but these basic necessities seem out of reach. It's okay to cry out to God and tell Him what you long for. Hiding in a cave from his enemies, David cried out in despair for God to rescue him (Psalm 142). David's prayers were finally answered but in God's timing and beyond his expectations.

This Christmas, as we hope for what we think is going to bring us satisfaction, and search to find answers for unfulfilled dreams, we can be comforted with these words in Isaiah. In the midst of disappointments, His word can be the power that makes your heart soar. Those who hope in Jesus will not be disappointed. In the tired and weary times, trust in the Lord and He will renew your strength. Praise God for you are His treasured possession (Exodus 19:5).

Lord God,

When we grow **T**ired and weary, we can **T**rust in Your **T**ender care. You work **T**irelessly, **T**eaching us as You **T**end to our every need. Life can be **T**urbulent and **T**reacherous but You are **T**imely with Your **T**remendous provisions and **T**houghtful understanding. We have been **T**ransformed by Your **T**enacious love. Our hearts are full of **T**hankfulness and we praise Your **T**riumphant name. Amen!

Questions:

1. What do you learn about God in today's devotional?

_____

_____

_____

2. What specific blessing can you thank God for this week?

_____

_____

_____

Reflections:

_____

_____

_____

_____

_____

Day 21

*U*NITING

"There is neither Jew nor Greek, slave nor free, male nor female, for you are all one in Christ Jesus." (Galatians 3:28)

This verse gives us assurance that by faith in Jesus Christ, we are united as children of God. There is no distinction between ethnicity or social position in God's family. Women are equal to men, and all are free in Jesus Christ. Is your identity as a mom, teacher, athlete, chef, artist, or secretary most important to you? Naturally, we feel more comfortable in our specific groups but no one group is better than another in Jesus' economy. We can be identified by many titles, but there is only one that matters.

The apostle John thought of himself as better than another when he tried to stop a man from driving out demons in Jesus' name. John thought the man had no right to do what he was doing because he wasn't part of the exclusive company of the twelve disciples. Jesus told

John not to stop the man. He proclaimed that whoever is not against you is for you (Luke 9:49-50). Our church affiliation might not be the same, but that doesn't mean we aren't doing God's work. There may be elements of disagreement but Jesus wants us to know we are equal and in a common relationship with Him.

We may be proud of our identity and our status in life, or we may feel inferior in a roomful of accomplished people. Our natural inclination is to define ourselves and become separated by our titles. The real issue is not "what" or "who" we are but Who we belong to. The good news is we are united and made one through Jesus Christ the newborn King.

Father,

We are so Underserving of Your Uniting love. We have been Unresponsive and Unappreciative of Your forgiveness. You desire to Unite Us. Through Your Undying love, we have everything we could ever need or want. Keep our hearts looking Upwards as You guide Us in the way we should go. Our feet can be Unsteady but You are our Unmovable Rock our ever present help in trouble. You Lord are like no other. Amen!

Questions:

1. What barriers do you need to remove to become more united with your church family?

_____

_____

_____

2. When describing yourself, what is most important and why?

_____

_____

_____

Reflections:

Day 22
Victorious

"I have been crucified with Christ and I no longer live, but Christ lives in me. The life I live in the body, I live by faith in the Son of God, who loved me and gave himself for me." (Galatians 2:20)

The apostle Paul reminds us that when we belong to Jesus our focus completely changes. We have a new commitment to follow Christ and a new purpose to live by faith. But how do we keep our focus on Christ in the midst of temptation and adversity?

Paul gives us his example of how he remained focused on Christ. He was abandoned, starved, stoned, thrown into prison, exposed to death again and again. He experienced physical, emotional and spiritual pressure and opposition on every side (2 Corinthians 11:23-27). Jesus' death and resurrection was Paul's guarantee that he was a deeply loved child of God. This truth gave him the strength to endure all of life's challenges. It was Paul's secret to a victorious life.

Even at Christmas it is not easy to remain centered on Christ. But like anything worthwhile, maintaining your focus will take persistence. Pray for understanding and wait expectantly for God to answer your prayer. Continue to study God's Word and surround yourself with like-minded Christians. There will be many setbacks and challenges, but don't give up. We have a lifetime to learn how to live by faith. Allow Jesus to fill every crevice of your heart and He will overflow into everything that you do and all that you think. You too will be able to join Paul and boldly say, "I can do everthing through Him who gives me strength" (Philippians 4:13). Experience this victory for yourself today!

Lord Jesus,

You have been **V**igilant in Your pursuit of us. We have been crucified with Christ. The life we live is **V**aluable because You have made us **V**ictorious in and through You. You are a true **V**isionary and we **V**ehemently praise Your holy name. Amen!

Questions:

1. What change can you make in your daily habits that will give you success in your thought life?

   _____

   _____

   _____

2. Where do you need to claim victory in Christ?

   _____

   _____

   _____

Reflections:

_____

_____

_____

_____

_____

_____

Day 23

WISE

"Then Samuel took a stone and set it up between Mizpah and Shen. He named it Ebenezer, saying, 'Thus far has the Lord helped us.'" (1 Samuel 7:12)

Samuel set a stone and named it Ebenezer, meaning stone of help to remind the Israelites of God's power and protection. Every time the Israelites saw the stone, they were reminded of God's faithfulness. For years, they had suffered under the hands of the Philistines. Samuel helped them to see God's hand in their challenges and accomplishments. Remembering God's past faithfulness helped them to trust Him in the present and it will do the same for us.

Think of a time in your life when you too waited for God's provision of help and guidance. You prayed consistently, but without evident answers you gave up. Like the Israelites, you became rebellious and defiant and pushed God away. Your hope was lost because you took your eyes off Jesus. Without Jesus as your guide, bumps in the road grew into mountains.

Don't let your present difficulties cloud your focus. Sin has a way of replacing truth with lies. Satan works to deceive us but all things are possible with God (Matthew 19:26). With Him no mountain is too big. When hope is lost, what is your visual reminder of God's faithfulness? To refocus, look to the cross, the manger, or another symbol that reminds you of God's presence. Look to Him for wisdom and make every effort to remember how the Lord has helped you in the past and you will be reminded you can trust Him in the present and in the future.

Wise, **W**ondrous Father,

Our faith has been known to **W**ain through life's challenges. We **W**ork to remain strong but on our own, we are **W**eak. We grow **W**eary and forget Your **W**isdom. We become **W**ayward and lost, but You are our **W**arrior. Your **W**atchful eye does not **W**aver from us. We are not alone. You love us **W**ithout measure. You are our guide and our protector. We **W**orship You and praise Your holy name. Amen!

Questions:

1. How have you experienced the Lord's faithfulness in the past year?

   _____

   _____

   _____

2. Who do you look to for advice and wisdom? Why?

   _____

   _____

   _____

Reflections:

_____
_____
_____
_____
_____

Day 24
eXcellent

"Finally brothers, whatever is true, whatever is noble, whatever is right, whatever is pure, whatever is lovely, whatever is admirable, if anything is excellent or praiseworthy, think about such things." (Philippians 4:8)

God wants us to know that it is important to focus our thoughts on that which is excellent or praiseworthy. When my daughter was young, she often had a difficult time getting back to sleep after waking from a bad dream. I would hold her in my arms and pray with her. In an attempt to relax her and get her mind off some particularly frightening thoughts, I would sing comforting songs and hymns till she fell back to sleep.

Middle school provided a whole different set of challenges. Between trying to fit in and the bullies that worked to destroy her self-esteem, she struggled to see good in herself and others. I wrote this verse on a card for her to take with her everywhere she went as a visual reminder of the importance of positive thinking.

Through prayer and continual focus on that which is praiseworthy and good she triumphed over the negativity surrounding her. To this day, she turns to these beautiful comforting words as she prays for strength and guidance.

Our Lord wants each of us to do the same. Instead of dwelling on what is wrong, our attention should be on whatever is true and right and admirable. Our government, the news, even our friends and families disappoint us. Rather than becoming angry and bitter, think about whatever is pure and lovely. And when tempted to raise ourselves or someone else to a position of honor, remember God alone is excellent and worthy of our praise. This Christmas and throughout the coming year, focus on our excellent Lord. Discover that Jesus alone is true, noble, right, pure, lovely, admirable, excellent and worthy of our praise.

Lord Jesus,

    Sadly, too often we focus on all the things that are wrong in our lives. We are in need of Your eXtravagant grace. Grant us an eXtra measure of patience and understanding both towards others and ourselves. Teach us to learn from Your eXample. Help us to focus on Your wonderful, ineXhaustible character. Fill us with Your Spirit of forgiveness as we practice this daily. In Jesus name we pray. Amen!

Questions:

1. Which Scripture verse can you memorize and write on an index card as a constant reminder of God's love for you?

    _____

    _____

    _____

2. What can you do to be more focused on what is true, right and admirable?

    _____

    _____

    _____

Reflections:

_____
_____
_____
_____
_____

Day 25
YEARNING

"On the last and greatest day of the Feast, Jesus stood and said in a loud voice, 'If anyone is thirsty, let him come to me and drink. Whoever believes in me, as the Scripture has said, streams of living water will flow from within him.' By this he meant the Spirit, whom those who believed in him were later to receive." (John 7: 37-39a)

In today's verse, Jesus promises streams of living water from within to those who believe in Him. He invites each of us to come to Him for refreshment that will last a lifetime. The water He offers does more than quench our thirst. Jesus further explains this in His encounter with the woman at the well. He promises her living water that will become a spring welling up to eternal life (John 4:10-14). The gifts under the tree will provide only temporary satisfaction. This gift from Jesus is the cure for spiritual thirst and brings life to an otherwise dead soul.

Do you recognize your need for the water Jesus is offering? Do you thirst for spiritual renewal and a deep satisfaction in Jesus? This verse tells us exactly what to do to receive Him. Come to Him, pray, confess and wait expectantly. Trust that when you seek Him, you will find His eternal thirst quenching water. Some days, we read, pray and meditate, but still feel empty. What do we do then? Be persistent and remember that Jesus yearns for us to come to Him and receive Him as Lord and Savior. Just as He gave this promise of living water to the Samaritan woman, He gives this promise to each of us searching for a deeper satisfaction that only a relationship with Him can give. Open yourself to Him and His life-giving Spirit and living water will fill your heart and refresh your soul with eternal renewal.

Yahweh,

Our hearts Yearn for Your life giving Spirit, but because of our selfish desires we struggle to Yield to Your calling. Come Lord Jesus, cleanse us from that which hinders Your Spirit's flow in us. Forgive us for Yesterday, and grant us the willingness and strength to say Yes, to You. In the coming Year may we Yield to Your streams of living water. In Jesus' name, Amen!

Questions:

1. Which suggestion will you use to experience daily spiritual renewal?

   _____

   _____

   _____

2. How can you implement that today?

   _____

   _____

   _____

Reflections:

_____

_____

_____

_____

_____

_____

Day 26

ZEALOUS

Jesus said, "For the Son of Man came to seek and to save what was lost." (Luke 19:10)

Simply stated, this verse defines Jesus' purpose on earth. Whole-heartedly, He was determined to do the will of the Father. And God's will is further explained in John 6:38-40. "For I have come down from heaven not to do my will but to do the will of him who sent me. And this is the will of him who sent me, that I shall lose none of all that he has given me, but raise them up at the last day. For my Father's will is that everyone who looks to the Son and believes in him shall have eternal life, and I will raise him up at the last day."

The Lord showed His determination to follow His Father's will as He called Zacchaeus down from a tree and invited Himself to his home (Luke 19: 5-6). He called Andrew and Peter as they were fishing and immediately they left their nets and followed Him

(Matthew 4: 18-20). Jesus zealously pursued and they gladly and immediately responded.

What's holding you back from responding to the Lord's call? Are you waiting for a specific answer to prayer? See Day #5 and be empowered. Do you feel unworthy? Turn to Day #6 and experience forgiveness. Are you afraid to take the first step? Refer to Day #16 and discover God's protection. He passionately pursues His children. Following Jesus and living a Christian life is not easy. But, it is possible to grow stronger as you walk in faith. Jesus is much more than our Christmas miracle. He's our Shepherd come to lead us home. He passionately pursues His children. What is your response to His call?

Lord God,

You are **Z**ealous for our love and attention. You patiently wait for us to quiet our minds and hearts so we can hear You. We **Z**ip through our days giving **Z**ero attention to the needs of those around us. Teach us to listen with our hearts. In Your most holy name, Jesus we pray. Amen!

Questions:

1. What have you learned about God's character through this study?

   _____

   _____

   _____

2. What is your understanding of God's purpose for your life?

   _____

   _____

   _____

3. What can you do to grow stronger as you walk in faith?

_____

_____

_____

Reflections:

_____

_____

_____

_____

_____

FOR FURTHER STUDY

1. Each day's reading begins with a theme verse taken from the New International Bible, copyright 2006. Explore this verse in The Message, King James Version or your version of choice for deeper understanding.

2. Look up passages recorded within each day and study the surrounding verses for context and meaning.

3. Refer to a Bible Commentary of your choice to further explore a topic or verse.

4. Ask yourself questions about what you have finished reading:

    a) How does this apply specifically to me?
    b) Why was this example important enough to be in the Bible?
    c) What will I do about what I read?

5. Memorize God's character traits:

    a) Practice recalling them in alphabetical order.
    b) Meditate on each one as you recite them aloud or silently to yourself.
    c) Use these attributes of God's character in your daily prayers and praise.

Verses by Day

1. 1 Corinthians 1:28-31; Luke 23:42-43; John 4:9; Romans 5:8

2. Revelations 3:1b-3

3. Isaiah 30:18; Genesis 6:14; Psalm 27:14

4. 1 Thessalonians 4:16-18; 2 Corinthians 1:3-5

5. 2 Thessalonians 1:11-12; Mark 11:25; Luke 6:12; Luke 11:1-13

6. Luke 23:34; Luke 22:54-62; John 20:24-28; Matthew 26:47-59

7. Ezra 7:21-23; 1 Corinthians 10:31; Matthew 25:23

8. Psalm 84:5-7; Zechariah 9:12

9. Ruth 1:14-16

10. Matthew 11:28-30; Genesis 22:13-14, 37:28-39:20, 50:20-21; Exodus 16:15; Matthew 4:11; Luke 22:43-44

11. Jeremiah 2:1-2; Exodus 13:21-22; Philippians 4:13; Ephesians 4:22-24

12. Joel 2:12-13; 1 Timothy 1:15-16

13. Deuteronomy 4:31; Genesis 21:1-5; 2 Samuel 11:1-17; Acts 13:22; Ruth 1:16; Matthew 1:5; Psalm 116:1

14. Jeremiah 31:3; Psalm 136; 1John 4:10; John 13:34-35

15. 2 Samuel 23:5

16. Isaiah 41:9-10; Genesis 3:10; Numbers 13; 1 John 4:18

17. Philippians 2:5-8; Matthew 27:12-14; Luke 23:9; John 13:4-17

18. Psalm 23:1-4; John 8:3-11; Ephesians 3:20

19. Isaiah 7:14; Matthew 1; Micah 5:2; Matthew 2:1-2; Hebrews 4:15; Luke 7:22

20. Isaiah 40:28-31; Psalm 142; Exodus 19:5

21. Galatians 3:28; Luke 9:49-50

22. Galatians 2:20; 2 Corinthians 11:23-27; Philippians 4:13

23. 1 Samuel 7:12; Matthew 19:26

24. Philippians 4:8

25. John 7:37-38a; John 4:10-14

26. Luke 19:10; John 6:38-40; Luke 19:5-6; Matthew 4:18-20

www.ingramcontent.com/pod-product-compliance
Lightning Source LLC
Chambersburg PA
CBHW021200210325
23867CB00012B/524